SHIFT

POEMS
MARYLEN GRIGAS

SHIFT

POEMS
MARYLEN GRIGAS

Nature's Face Publications

Shift ~ Poems
Copyright 2016 by Marylen Grigas

All rights reserved. No part of this book may be used or reproduced in any manner whatsoever without written permission except in the case of brief quotations embodied in critical articles and reviews.

Cover image by Jeremy Fortin
Author photo by Jeremy Fortin
Book design by Lindsay Francescutti

ISBN: 978-0-9829004-8-2

Nature's Face Publications
106 Shore Acres Drive
Colchester, Vermont 05446

For all my family and friends

Contents

I

Shift 3
About Muscle 4
Foreign Cities 5
The First Cell: Longing 7
First Division 9
At Leda Lanes 12
Bricolage 13
In and Out of the Livery of the Passion 15
Running Dog 18
Earth: An Introduction to Planet Creation 20
Dear William Carlos Williams 21
Ars Poetica 22
Ode to the Corpus Callosum 24
Arrival 25
Syntax Me, Please..26
Installation 28
Caution   Train Is Crossing   Train Is Crossing 30
Root 31

II

Whiteout..35
Waiting...37
Clytemnestra at Home...38
Re: Household Tips..39
Song...40
Night Mending...41
Habitats...42
The Sum of its Parts..43
Breakfast to Bed...45
Aubade with Fog..47
The Oracle Replies...48
Notes from a Capricious Correspondent..........................49
Stanzas with Symptoms..50
Folding..52
At My Father's Desk..54
A Hypochondriac's Guide to the Body.............................56
Home Security...57
Origins..58
Particles at a Distance...60
Package...62
Sunday's Children...63
New England Summer..64

III

Hatch 67
Flame 69
Waking to Grief 70
East Woods 71
Looking up from bleak headlines at these friable trees 72
April Accounting 73
You Will Feel a Pinch 74
Prayer 75
What the Rock Said 76
While you were sleeping 77
Questions While Deep-Cleaning the Desk 79
More Gray 82
Hammocked and Unstrung 83
Story 85
Windblown Sonnet for Brass 86
Free Will with Small Yellow Truck 87

Acknowledgments 89

I

I

Shift

      watch   listen   something-just-arrived
is missing   like a larch that's dropped its golden leaves
      sudden somehow

      gone with taxicab-yellow rushing
though you believe
      what's missing must be

      must be time   lack of time hangs heavy
a thick gold watch on a choke chain
      left in the back seat of a yellow cab rushing away

      something's missing   there go its tail lights
you can hear its lowering whine   but then
      it's leafing gold again   loud and lush and leafing

      time unlocking its effects once more:
watches   lives   leaves intentions misplaced keys
      startling abundance   amplitude

      yet in all this high-pitched yellow   how could it be
this urgency   faint alarm   this expectancy
      easy   easy

About Muscle

If there's no need for movement, then no need for a brain, I've learned,
a fact demonstrated by the sea squirt, a small creature that swims
freely in its youth until it settles on a rock. Then it devours its own brain.
And spinal cord. It simply doesn't require them any longer.
(God, don't let me settle.) Need for movement leads to need for muscle.
The brain evolves in order to plan and execute reaching, grasping,
turning, according to the expert on *Charlie Rose*, which I watch
on my iPad while walking on the treadmill to rebuild my strength.
Plenty of species thrive without brains, he says. It could be different
on another planet, I suppose, but here evolution of the brain is about muscle.
Just ask Arnold Schwarzenegger or an evolutionary biologist.
Yet the brainless sea squirt still gets upset, still squirts.
Maybe it's innate, like a horse's hide shuddering to dislodge a fly.
Maybe that's why I started moving and arranging boulders last fall.
I thought I was making a terrace. But afterward it looked more like a grave.

Foreign Cities

I've heard it said that death is a hazy passage
but why not something more definitive, not a loosening

of consciousness, a letting go, shavasana, the dead man's pose
with shallow breath, cells shutting down their failing businesses,

pulling the blinds, turning the signs to *closed*, but rather a flash of light
and it's 1908, long before you were born, when sweating horses

pulled dripping ice carts down dirt streets, grocery cart following
the rag man, cleaned rags in front, dirty in back,

yet questions of consciousness linger, all this learning,
all this striving, all this becoming—years spent clambering up

each new experience, endless days of school gazing toward
the next season, dreams of traveling to foreign cities, where you

might suddenly be released into real life and its sweet clarity,
a movie in which the director no longer shouts to turn this way

or that, but releases you to your own inner certainty, a compass
which, after all, has been silently turning since those days

you were floating in a womb, and now you feel its swing
toward magnetic north, you feel the weight of the planet,

you sense movement, its spinning fire and shooting rays
like hands of Shiva, through you, through the planet,

through the Milky Way, through deep space to its beginning,
when the first cell split into longing.

The First Cell: Longing

I am oneness,
single
within a snug wall,
that took
billions of years
to build.
That fashioned self.

I want.
I move toward.
Through warm streams,
currents, gentle and harsh,
currents within me
and without
in constant flow.

I am the unaided eye.
Later, both predator and prey.
Later, enfolder and enfolded
near you, on you, in you,
in dust, stars and constellations.

Grown old and worn,
mighty vibrations wrench
until I am asunder.
You, my progeny,
you will want more
yet long for me–
Blessed Singularity.

First Division

When the men drag a hose into the flames
on the second floor of the meat packing plant,
a flash fire greets them
and the fat-soaked floor where my father's men are standing
explodes and caves.

Zukoski, Stevens, Pelletier, Tessier

drop to the fire below. Three crawl out. Stevens is missing.
No ladders raised yet, my father
throws the fire hose over the window ledge—
a makeshift escape route for the three and goes back in.

> I am second oldest of five in a family of seven
> seven divided by one is always seven.
> The next to the youngest clings to Mother in the roped-off crowd.
>
> I have been learning the rules of division, what is divided
> from what, the fearful sound of the word *what what*
> windy beginning and frozen end.
>
> *What* is the product or result.
> *He has come out once and will come*
> *once more*, Father Jonas says next to me, *one more time.*

Stevens calls from below and my father feels his way down —
he is the second oldest of eight crawling through space

through flames toward Stevens, whose dead weight is hefted up,
whose black coat seals with his own,
the rubbery surface singeing his face.

    the rules are easy
    how many times can one
    thing be contained in another

Seared, almost silent, the men in a row of five beds —
Zukoski, Stevens, Pelletier, Tessier, Grigas

dressings and painkillers
                        wives and children
                                          the sacraments
the body and blood   unrecognizable faces
                float in and out like consciousness

between the before and the after what is left
        is seldom the same
                the heap of uniforms smolders on the hospital floor.

His face will burn pink in cold weather, and if we turn on a light
in the darkened living room where he sits by the window,
he will startle and we will apologize.

Years later on his death bed, when a nurse flashes a light on him,
he will sit up, place his feet into the space
where his boots should be.

At Leda Lanes

Bowling to rock and roll at the new Leda Lanes
(girls are an *occasion for sin* in such a place,
Sister Agnes has scolded) we rejoice,
drinking sodas, eating devil dogs,
reading *Brave New World* aloud between sets.
Grown men sporting ducktails eye us,
call us *chicks* and wink, stare blatantly at our breasts.

We flirt back as we slam heavy plastic balls
against bald pins, keeping score with bird-foot slashes.
We're singing out of tune when one of the men bends to bowl.
When his muscled forearm emerges from his denim sleeve,
a tattooed snake uncoils with his thrust of the ball.
But then his Elvis toupee slips down his nose.

We snicker at his blush as he glances toward us.
My friend's long fingers cup her ball
as if it holds the future.
Merciless, she unwinds and strikes.

Bricolage

Grandmother built a patio
with remnant stones.
Cobbled together a shed
from scavenged boards.
Broad-shouldered Baltic
built for heavy burdens,
her identity concealed in the drone
of distraction. Long before the camps
that took her neighbors,

she was hidden in the folds
of Blessed Mother's cloak–
now living in the third person,
one with a furrowed brow,

like a beast of burden,
lathered, stolid, solid,
pulling forward.
A beast delivered bawling
in a land of farmers
whose instinct to survive
on shrewd meagerness and
careful invisibility saved them.

She picked worms off cabbages,
repainted the wheelbarrow, hammers, hoes
daubed with fading camouflage,

gathered hodgepodge rules and rectitude
like ingredients for a stew
and pieced together a borrowed god from scraps,
then placed it at a crossroad.

In and Out of the Livery of the Passion

1. Red Scapular

Two-sided leather frames
held icons of Madonna and Child,
a promise of relief from pain,
lungs aflame in a sickly child.

Clad in the livery of the passion,
I slid in and out of the river of fire —
first body, then soul,
scapular hanging from a woolen cord

my mother placed there
beneath my white cotton shirt
sweating the front and back of my heart.
Sacred hearts pierced, one with a sword,
the other a crown of thorns.

A lesson in how pain clarifies, purifies,
melding with the wounded hearts
of Madonna and Child of affliction.

2. Ockham, Excommunicate

Exiled by his own sharp tongue,
he lay beneath the gambrel slant
of a foreign attic room
where moonlight
casts for trout
on the opposing wall.

Each night he prayed:
Free me from false heresy
from priests who would
elaborate their habits,
deny simplicity, analysis,
his passion.

But at night here was All:
the cross revealed
in the roof's shadows,
the familiar leaping
in his chest,
the clean curve of that fish.

3. Anchorman

At first I wanted to say something about love.
Nothing borrowed, beribboned.
Nothing blue. My brother's gaze locked
on the hospital's overhead television.
He is anchored to the anchorman
and his weirdly intermingled stories–
of beheadings and strip mall Santas,
Saint Nicholas lost in traffic
with the rest of his early devotions.
He is anchored to this life,
no matter the content, even when
there is nothing but strip mall air
in oversized, gaudily wrapped boxes.
Commercial break. I try a station with chimes.
He scowls. His grandchild does a card trick.
He smiles. He's refused the sacrament of Extreme Unction.
Instead he desires ice on his tongue,
would love a glimpse of clouds, more CNN news,
savoring each moment's ticking, each labored breath.
He will cling to life like a leach to the multiplied fish.

Running Dog

It wasn't a subtle variety of truth I wanted then
but a blunt-nosed dog crashing through the den
a dog stupidly earnest and inelegant
scattering books, fringed lampshades
carrying away a comfortable old shoe

I wanted an ungainly bicycle, swerving
through a curve, heart leaping, a swirl of gravel
rising around my ankles, nothing symmetrical

I wanted the crash of atoms in an accelerator
wrecking the rule that truth can't be grasped
a molten equation spewing from a hillside
its foliage on fire, a rain of ash dispelling
all blurry postulates, obscuring the sunset
but not the running dog

Concerning the Nature of Inquiry

These days I love a question with a blue tattoo.
Appealing with its inky consistency:
rosebud, yes, or dove, but not a chain link fence.

Once I wanted a question with a fill-in-the-blank answer.
Better yet, multiple choice: a) bird gripping a gray day
b) demagogue's pursed lips c) Canada

I don't care for questions in masks, but I'd try one
with a thrown voice, or maybe one disguised as a survey.

But never a question filled with down,
its answer—nothing but feathers in the throat.
Politicians can either uplift or gag.

No duck-blind questions need apply
or any that coo, *Come, I will lead you*....
Even psychopaths love their dogs.

Earth: An Introduction to Planet Creation

To the Middle Schooler From a Far More Advanced Planet Who is Running this Experiment: Please tweak my left lung and save Syria. Otherwise, we can't go on–don't you see the signs? I'm serious about Syria–unless like many of Earth's kids your age and much older, you like to see things blow up. Are you taking a wait-and-see attitude? Please don't, but show us how to use our big brains and struggling hearts. Maybe you did start the whole project wrong, but I think it can be corrected. No need to erase us and start over. Ask your teacher for help. Here's an old idea– cooperation instead of competition. Pump that up. We've tried that here on a small scale. Really. And the results? How about the Volvo…made by teams of satisfied workers. How about our commune in Sheldon? No, scratch that. The worst meetings I've ever attended. Everyone talking at once, grandstanding. Oh, and here's a question I'd wish you'd ask your teacher. Please ask why you multiply mass by the speed of light squared. Squared? It's always seemed arbitrary to me, and no one you've created has ever been able to explain it convincingly. In simple language, please. Another thing. Why do I suddenly want to know everything about William Carlos Williams? Everything.

Dear William Carlos Williams

*"so much depends / upon / a red wheel /
barrow / glazed with rain / water / beside the white / chickens."*

For my 4-H chicken project, a good pastime
for a sickly, asthmatic child, my grandfather built me a red wheelbarrow
with removable sides. On the front he emblazoned
"Wild Bill" in mustard yellow. Not a reference to you, William,
 but to the cowboy. I loved cowboys.

We lived on the other side of town. I loved chickens, too.
But perhaps you didn't *love* them at all or the red wheelbarrow.
But if not, then why would so much depend upon them?
I believe your white chickens were Bantams,
like the ones I raised.

I removed Soldier, the smallest and weakest rooster, from the coop
to protect him from bullying. At night he slept in a basket
in our cellar. Free to roam, Soldier walked with a peculiar
stiff-legged gait. My wheelbarrow is disintegrating
in the back yard now, Soldier long dead.

Maybe they weren't your own chickens or wheelbarrow.
Yet arching over us all, the same chilly stars, through us, neutrinos.
We know that now. And all this particulate in the airways,
Dr. Williams, makes it hard for me to breathe.
Did any of your white chickens have names?

Ars Poetica

After all that chewing, digesting,
as if each sound were cellulose,
there's a tightening behind the ears,
not a worrisome tightening as in the chest
or the rustle of chewing in the walls,
but a pleasant compression, a small band

improvising a dance tune just for you.
Company may come, or company may not,
no matter—there's that tightening of intention
so that you find yourself invigorated, single-minded,
quickly picking up clothes from the floor

where they were dropped, putting away the dishes,
wiping down the counters,
since maybe this is what needs to be done—
as critical as wildly dancing alone in the kitchen
because isn't extreme messiness a symptom
of excessive carelessness, a loosening of focus?

Then wouldn't we be milling around
with serious lack of intention—like termites?
Although they can, come to think of it,
even in all their milling,
finally and without leadership or direction,
build a nest like a cathedral,
probably to their great surprise.

Ode to the Corpus Callosum

Across the hemispheres, images thirst
for words that bring news,

fresh pour from a mountain stream,
and words on the other side crave icons,

embers carried back and forth across
the Pyrenees by fleet-footed messengers

as Thisbe and Pyramus whisper lovers' plans
through the precious chink in the wall.

Mirrored sparks flicker along deep canyons,
across rivers of flotsam, when a soft-breathed

sense of self emerges from foam on the river,
from clean air in the mountain pass.

Creation in its minutest specks is delivered,
and the infant turns to the mother's voice,

the whale to a rumble of song
the mouse to a scatter of crumbs.

Arrival

As if life depends on it, a wobbling first impression
slips from alpha through rays of particles
hunting for its anchor.

Bambi-faced, it asks *Are you my mother?* Bounces
a ball beneath the table where a thousand angels
curl through smoke rings a gambler blows.

Departs from that hall diced and carded
through the smeared letterhead of gods
on their way to bed, their worn robes flapping.

Out into the world, enlightened, wind-blown
surprised at its own being
it calls out like a gull crying *Here!*

Right here! Such a racket a newborn makes
as it stretches, gobbles its fist, searches for sustenance,
reaches for more.

Syntax Me, Please

Please. Clear up or confirm my confusions.
Do so in a new and appealing way.
Tighten me, but keep me true
because here at home spring
is bringing forth its punch list
so time contracts and chores expand.

Loosen me, a low-cut voice
in a new and appealing way.
Black and diaphanous. Off
with the workman's gloves.
Quickly, please, my confusions.
I've heard light is both
particle and wave,
but not till today
did I learn that slug slime
is both lubricant and glue.
I admit I don't know
what to make of it.

I can tell you, though,
they say meaning
is mostly in the syntax,
the core and *haut couture*
of expression. Oh, but where

does the mystic lie,
and what makes it stick,
in this deluge of information,
this reign of style? I'll
clean my prose of garden soil.
Polish my nails like stanzas.
I appeal to you. My confusions.
In writing, please.

Installation

Three arcs of lights hang from the museum wall
        and drape across the floor of an otherwise empty room.
                A necklace of diamonds for a larger-than-life empress?
Has the Empress left with her lover in the aftermath
        of a disappointing Christmas? After all,
                look down at your own stockings, filled only with feet.
Perhaps the artist died in transit from the subway?
        Synapses flash like Christmas lights, but no arc
                of meaning is delivered to the station.
Has the Empress thrown herself beneath a train?
        Long live the Empress!

My reflection stares back at me in a hundred silent lights.
        Observer observed by the observer. Blurred.
                And here rococo as an Egon Schiele.
My own face an expressionist portrait
        (another section on the second floor)
                but out of place here, out of sync,
                        my face, with its dripping interiority.

Three feet apart, each end held up
        by titanium bolts against the white wall.
            Meta-materialism, I think, or Meta-realism. Three strands
of light bulbs (are they sixty watts?) hang from the white wall.
        (Hanging, but nothing to do with saints or criminals.)
           Three arcs of light hang (or droop, or rest, or sag)
out onto the floor for a foot or so. And that is that.

In this room it does not rain frogs or fish.
        No flowers, animals, maps. Just as a traveler
           comes to a distant land where people speak
an unknown language, yet someone gestures,
        Come sit with us. Here, eat, drink!

           so, too, this foreign room might, but instead
stares blankly, reflecting otherness.
        Empress! Come home, please. Tell me a story
           of what's kept you, even if it's not true.

Caution   Train Is Crossing   Train Is Crossing

Waiting at the crossing for a backing train, its lambent
graffiti, luminous letters strange in this barn-red town, ambient
in the Bronx or Brooklyn maybe, or wherever they were born; have they been

sent to inform of change with the words KRAZY KEY III in such peculiar shades?
Letters zag WILDCHILD BABES, SUPER SKULLS above a bubbly red HADES.
Words wield KID KONG, WIKED160, and magenta scraped to mustard over black adds

PHASE 2 in circles and cones. What's coming? From the wheels to the roof stretches
STITCH like a coiled snake roiling around striped ZIBRA, stunned by its treacherous
beauty. Potent prefigurement in multiple layers, so boldly compelling, it reaches

into our brains: JESUS CHRIST, JESSE JAMES. REACT it reads roundly as it crashes
together, squeals forward; FLASH it shouts loudly in colors of Oldenburg, Rausch-
enberg, Johns. In this town here from some city there, it whispers: ashes, ashes, ashes.

Root

Weighty, my *American Heritage,*
yet *shillyshally* springs lightly
from its belly when my shaky hand
riffles for some escape from my latest fright–
news flash of mistaken drone strike
or the nightmare that woke me–
to lists of calming possibilities
with their long and serious histories.

I want to hide behind a word like a wall,
a word that never trembles, panics, never freezes
as we did that time we were *collateral* damage
on a street of financiers' mansions
standing in the middle of a dreamscaped lawn
where we could no longer fight,
couldn't even shout *Power to the people,*
when we simply wanted to lie down and rest.
Co laterally. *Com latus. Come lie by my side.*
Forlorn.

I wonder how it is those Alaskans on the news
remain so calm and stalwart,
even when at this moment one quarter mile
of the main road has been avalanched
with forty feet of snow. In response, backhoes

and forty feet of *fortitude*. (Old-fashioned term
weakened as it meandered from its strong root.
From *fortis*, from *fort*, with its unbreachable stone walls
built stone by stone by multitudes of men.)

Alaskans, though, are ready, fighter-pilot calm—
like my young friend's dad
up in a dark jet above the stadium
guarding the Super Bowl against terror
while, below, a football player place-kicks,
steady and certain. Such a difference between *tiger*
and *tiger beetle*, flashing its delicate shield, running
so fast the world becomes a blur.

II

Whiteout

Deep winter, the three of us driving in an old van home

from a party. Toddler on my lap, his mémère's knitted hat,

its pom poms brushing my cheek.

Through his hand-me-down snowsuit, the sweetness

of our sleepy child's compact warmness. We are slipping away

from an impending heartbreak, wreckage.

Back through the lowlands in a whiteout,

dim lights of an occasional farmhouse.

Going home. Imagining forgiveness.

Husband concentrating on the snowy road—

a curving white rope through a conifer forest

when our child points, cries out over careful conversation

and the blast of the heater: "I see a whiteness hopping!"
We swerve. The snowshoe hare crosses in front of us
and into the woods. A blur. We believe we're okay.

Even from a distance we're convinced that we're visible
here below in the trees. The rope of road pulls us back onto our course.
The white night leaps forward with its powerful back legs.

Waiting

You think me a feeble girl? Do you know who I am?
—Clytemnestra, wife of Agamemnon

My mind scans the horizon, launches
                swift ships of reconnaissance.
Such constant vigilance has strained my eyes, creased my forehead,
                so much squinting into the glare of possibilities.
I purse my lips, breathe life into dust
                and curl into the nest of my name,
exploding from its feathered center,
                I'm blind as justice to everything but rage.

                Watching from the front lawn,
where from miles away his headlights are discernible,
                I wait for them to disappear behind a hillock,
then to flare up and over these stubbled waves of corn.
                Something quiet and ragged is nesting in my rib cage,
and when I shift my burden
                like a fevered toddler from one raw hip
to the other, even a sudden shower
                of blossoms burns my skin.

I think me a feeble girl.

Clytemnestra at Home

At first, it was as if my days were suspended. A sense
of constriction overcame me. After a while, I felt compelled

to walk to the sea, stare out until my eyes ached,
scan for returning ships, as if I were eager.

Well, it wasn't constriction exactly, more a self-imposed ache,
but now, simply an opening and a list of tasks.

Cloth to be woven, the filthy floor. I could stand
to send my lover away, no matter what anyone says.

Sometimes it seems the fates have overlooked me.
Or not. So let them spin, measure, let them snip.

And rather than a measure of time filling me, I fill time.
What with sheep to shear, children to feed, my ax to grind.

Re: Household Tips

For your incontinent fifteen-year-old Italian Greyhound: beneath his newspapers place the glossy pages of the Sunday *New York Times Style Magazine–Aruba… sublime interiors…San Miguel.* They repel the pee and protect the floor.

For water leaks: use big buckets or small bowls, depending. Place a paper towel in the small bowl to avoid splashing the furniture. And a plastic bag beneath the bowl to protect the couch.

For a poem that won't work: stop and pat the dog. Forget about the poem.
For your frazzled brain: work a Sudoku puzzle until it is illegible with erasure.

For your aunt who thinks her refrigerator is spewing poisonous gases: put food in it one day, then eat it in front of her the next. Pickles are quick and easy.

(*Wait a minute, Whiner, couching your complaints in the guise of household tips. Look, you're not being swept away in a tsunami, nor attacked by rats,*

nor overcome by the smell of burning wires and leaking Freon. It's easy to be flippant when your household doesn't tip and spin with fear….)

If pickles don't convince, try blueberry pie with vanilla ice cream or maybe…

(*Okay, you've slipped again. You didn't come clean. That wasn't a retraction, no honest apology for unkind wit, now was it? And admit it! It turns out the fridge has a faulty fan. Try again.*)

Soon your roof will be restored…and your dead sister sends only happy reports.

Song

Red bird, spark in the leafless fire bush,
when the world turns flat, and white nothing

swallows every other vivid thing, you don't succumb,
you with your *pretty girl, pretty girl*, that endless song.

Once I was a shop girl who hung red dresses
on limbs of an apple tree in the heart of winter.

Laughing over my shoulder, I led a lover to a house
on a dead-end road. In the distance, white birches

threaded up through a darkness of their own making.
We became foreshortened shadows in noon sun.

Now look at me, silent and hollow as a plastic saint,
the phone ringing up its days of obligations.

Stroll away, stroll away, you sing.
But here we stay.

Night Mending

Pick up your raveling hem, make stitches
neat and even.
                       Scan for
torn edges inside and out,
                do your best to patch the damage.

When distress makes you wobble, sense
                           the four corners of each foot.
When you feel only three,
          realize that triangles call for resolution,

pull the night in three directions, so that one corner

        remains untucked, exposes fault lines
that can't be breached,

                 whole gaping years of ripped and fallen things,

innocence, like a moth in an unblemished cloak,
                yellow and brick against apple and leaf.

Mend, mend, until the first star of morning.

Knock mind against what it might fix,
      what's scarred, what it can't undo.

Habitats

You can take Vermont,
the edge of the woods in tears
even with spring's sky-blue gown

as you prowl through those trees
bird whistle on a lanyard and compass
tucked in your camouflage pants.

I want Montana for myself,
some little-known hot spring,
glimpse of wild horses running,

notebooks, novels, no plans
as the sky rolls out its
dazzling welcome mat.

Just a long flat highway with nothing
at stake between us.

Someday we'll signal one another—
you with the call of a partridge,
me with the song of a meadowlark.

The Sum of its Parts

He says he's felt
time snag like silk
through his hands

the night that lurched
from a mountain road
and crashed over them

the time her name
slipped from his tongue
a name he'd have
carved into cliffs

She reminds him
of each day that
lingered lighthearted

afternoons handed
back and forth
like a bubble

Each hour that spilled
like a weasel
into its burrow

delicate head
long white hide
black-tipped tail

Breakfast to Bed

Opening the door to reach for the paper,
I'm struck by this morning's sharpness:
how sun spotlights the snow banks,
curves the culverts, cuts to the curbed street.

Even the headlines glare. War again.
It's a day with teeth.
In the kitchen I slice bread
while a pan of butter bubbles on the stove.
Certainly today anything unclear will sink.

My little boy pulls on his boots,
picks up his backpack–Ready. Set.
The dialectic of day whirls us in its bucket–

All day I listen to the undersides of words,
treat wounds, invent temporary solutions.
Until late afternoon's dusk begins to pull us
to ourselves, and slow-talking

we take long-shadowed strides
to our lake with its iced broil of sun,
where a bronze general, hand on hilt,
guards the southern approach.

Soon night begins to breathe
just behind the ear
as streetlights take up their watch.

Dishes cleared. At the kitchen table
the boy plies his sharpened pencil,
writing a story from breakfast to bed,

a story wearing a cloak of armies
massing at the border. *Then the general
leads his army to fight. Then the enemy flees.*

I listen to some late night station
fuzzy with distance and wind.
The family is safe at home, he's written,
Then the family sleeps.

Aubade with Fog

Little whirling gods both here and not here–
Maybe piquant coffee wafts aromas
from some sunny Puerto Rican hillside
in this chilly kitchen north of Boston
where a fog horn droned on and off all night.
Maybe a small girl asks, "Mama, is that the moon or sun?"
Morning light comes late in hazy ribbons
yellow as the egg yolks in the coddling kettle
that might have hatched like red-winged plans of blackbirds
murmured on some distant dreaming planet
where grosgrain rivers meander dark and lustrous.
Maybe a small girl yawns as you brush
her auburn hair, matted as a nest of baby starlings,
beaks stretched open at the slightest stirrings.

The Oracle Replies

Because of the hornet in my chest, its needling discomfort
in this vaporous cave echoing with argument.

The distracting murmur of my own need:
to be embodied, to bend to a sheaf, to a lover.

So often it is only the hornet where my heart should be
who follows their pleading eyes, gesturing hands—
the frightened and deluded don't seem to hear its buzzing.

Because I am a conduit from the earth's vast liver
and when I open my cavernous mouth, a swarm
of imperfect directions is released:

I say *Walk backwards down this road until you can see the present.*
I say *Walk inland until you recognize yourself in someone's face.*
I want to say *Soften into your sorrow, soften.*

Notes from a Capricious Correspondent

Through half-shut blinds above the filling tub,
    Morning illuminates vapors of steam,
        a fantasia of gold-leafed lemons,

bright and sudden as coins
    pulled from a magician's sleeve,
        a mere mixture of water and dust.

Next a burlesque—sheerest silk veils shimmy
    across my sulky mirrored face,
        when by subtle indirection,

another beam gathers its soulful skirts and rolls
    in the roundness of the porcelain sink,
        as if being hand washed and gently squeezed

by some invisible Nereid. *Step into the bath*, she insists,
    let your tangled hair stream around you.
        Float.

Stanzas with Symptoms

Did you say lobectomy or
        lobotomy? Of the lung
or of the brain? Both
        frequent family flyers:
spiraling genes
        set down
down with gin and guns
        down with bad lungs
with misfiring brains
        down with twists of
barbed wire to catch
        a bird singing
songs for the unselected.

World of rain, rot, and restoration
        World of tip and tilt
of tropical storms:
        Sister's psychotropics and their side effects–
tollus of the neck-contorted agony
        head cocked down and to the side.
Pain exchanged for seclusion in a quiet mind.
        Pruners long ago gone in and whacked the circuits.
Clocks tick tick tick in every room.

       World of upside down and sideways
World of askance and askew
       chance and charge:
Who's in charge here? Cells wild and
       alliterating in the alleys of my lungs—
beserkers looting, biting their own shields,
       setting fires to villages, to any living thing.

Dear world, whirl, and wind:
       dizzying and dangerous as
promises online
       for weight loss, laser vision
but no one can fix her frazzled heart,
       her burnt circuitry
or the wildfire in my lungs.

Folding

She folds and refolds her obsessions,
impatience blinking like a walk sign
above her grandmother's cross-stitched towels.

She works quickly, her daughter
already stamping her foot at the wall of her womb,
her small son stirring from a restless nap.

Built by her great-grandfather, passed down
a treacherous line, the chest is never full,
its contents slowly shift, like her drive for perfection.

Not even her numerous attempts absolve her.
Not a handful of cheerfully pink erasers.
Not her grandmother's comb, her father's fire helmet,

her uncle's rosary beads. Her temper.
She looks for anything to smother
the hourly confusions.

In the depression at the center
is a burrow with miles of tunnels
hard to follow as a hare in snow.

She stuffs her trembling into one end
of her mother's white rabbit muff.
It disappears like hands.

At My Father's Desk

His provenance: suspicion
that a half-truth carries a half-life.
He gave me flabbergast

and my habitual questioning.
What's the story here? he'd ask
with no expectation of an answer
as my sister and I tussled.

Still, my firefighter father was
first into any burning building.

Sent away at seven
by his immigrant family
to pick beans, slop pigs.
My father of flummox
gave me flummox.

I'm stunned by the certainty
of declarative sentences, speechless
before their imperious assurance.

Tonight, behind his desk's pull-out pillars,
in secret spaces large enough
for a dozen thin documents,
I find nothing but thin air

when what I want
are yellowed letters filled
with declarations of remorse
from other generations.
But it's late, it's night
and I stand here staring
the way a deer stares
when her legs have forsaken her.

A Hypochondriac's Guide to the Body

Never mind discussing what is and isn't postmodern, let's discuss post nasal, let's disgust ourselves for the better good of our bodies—minds are another matter. I've just read a poem describing the symptoms of someone's mother. She has faded, but her symptoms remain emblazoned on the back of my esophagus. No amount of coughing helps. Could it be *can- can-* can't say it, but chances are good that it is, society riddled with it at every level, so why not? Even my hound continues to woo woo whine for more meat, while his colon only accepts rice. How does motion affect the body? A sixteen-mile bike ride leaves ailments in the dust, the dust left in the dust, dust full of dander, pollen, mites and mold. All those skin tests for allergens, seeing them all light up, all the components of planet Earth. Where does the mind fit in? That, too, has its symptoms. Perhaps we're a foolish lot in the absence of pain and worry, wasting our time searching for nutritional yeast. Get back on your bike, follow the road until it disappears into a crowd of days and into the underbrush, fraught with *ifs* and their spiky leaves—some poisonous, some medicinal, some both.

Home Security

Like one possessed, the man I love is building a home security system,
using his recovered electrical engineering skills
to make us safe. So many break-ins in our neighborhood lately.
So many need drug money.

How do cells sound their alarms? My last test imaged cells flashing red.
Gobbling sugar, they glowed red. Four zones in this house,
trips back and forth to Radio Shack,

bringing out dusty electronics–switches, relays, magnetic sensors–
pushing tiny wires through passages, winding them
around minute screws. Red warns danger.

Nobody will get in. His engineering notebook
open to his schematic drawing beautifully rendered and certain.
Now he's drilling holes in the floors of each room to run the wires.
Not even the smallest intruder can slip in.

Origins

Was it the slam of an open hand or a fist
that crushed millions of angels dancing on the head of a pin–
their mouths tiny startled o's?

That was powerful enough to smash energy
smaller than a pinprick, infinitely compressed
into a dust storm, infinitely large–

Or was it a long, loud exhalation to be sucked back
into some colossal lung?

And we wee ones–subjects and objects–
all of us doing things, with all of everything–
to be destroyed again

before we've had time to–
O, just even time to–

Once when wind slammed the door shut,
I startled awake and shouted, "Help!"

"Why do you always call for help?" he asked.
"O, I don't," I retorted, "Sometimes I say fur,

sometimes feathers."
But this is no time for nonsense.

I need to know for my report to the authorities–
Which was it–open hand or fist?

Particles at a Distance

When two particles are entangled, they retain a connection even when separated over great distances, so that actions performed on one affect the other.
— Clara Moskowitz, *Scientific American*, 12/11/13

What love and grief are circling–
    Who's there?

Beneath vertiginous stars,
she watches and deliberates–

the air above burns with hazardous afterlife.
    What feverish origin?

How close or far need one be
    to feel another's gravity?

Impossibly entwined.
    All chance of change

rapt and dark.
    Intimate and infinitesimal circling–

Just what is *this* circumstance?
    Why when the circler whirls on one toe,

the stander a universe away
        feels dizzy.

Always impossible for us to be unmoved
        when a spirit spins us,

when we hear the broken breath,
        that calling out. *Who's there?*

Package

Sad sad wrapped in anxious anxious,
wrapped in a slew of questions;

Shrink wrapped in a warped frame,
still wishing for connections....

Even with weather mild and kind,
even with new romantic dreams

and dimly lit rooms,
my mind recoils:

Not anchors, not answers
not icons or echoes,

but just a thin strap
would do.

Stars above burn in their constellations,
Dog Star wrapped with a white dwarf;

white dwarf bound in gravity,
Dog Star the axis of it all,

even as every sad and limping thing
collapses and radiates.

Sunday's Children

Out on a day like Pavarotti's voice, a jogger, spandexed and snappy, slaps past.
I stop fast-walking at the light, where a heavy truck jakebrakes. Its kettle drum
compression delivers a sucker punch to the stomach. Heavy metal from
its open window twangs, "Whataya whanna whanna do?" Then a cloud of exhaust.

Ahead, Felix lights up on the corner of Lyman, and checks the sky like a watch.
The sky is heavy as lead pipes. He sings his daily song of crossroads, Lyman or Pine?
Shaky hands. *Tardive dyskinesia* and a tattered book of matches. If one, it's Lyman,
if two, then east. Day by day, he's curling up like a slow burning match.

"West wind, west wind," he sings. He fumbles with his headphones.
Then something like *Gumos kaip tu batas. Just like a rubber boot,* he says. *Crazy.*
Felix takes a drag and heads east to the new mall that sprawls in the lap of the city.
Heading for the lake path, I am hoping for a cheerful interlude, hoping for

a joyful non sequitur, a mother pushing a laughing child in a red stroller. I know the law
of averages is far superior to our expectations. I know happy is as happy does.
Lake spray laps my legs with its blithe tongue. Under my feet the path softens. A breeze
wraps itself around my shoulders. The day clears it throat, then begins another aria.

New England Summer

Stand very still
by this frost-heaved stone wall,
watch swallow-shouldered, fleet and sudden
June swerve into moonfaced
July: such sleek brown stretching
long limbed, so whitebellied
and limber over morningdewed clover.
Hold on
as tremblenosed, busymouthed
July is seized by lame and wheezing
August, its yellowed teeth and ragweed breath,
its raspy throat and ochre hints of cold;
this sting of August, this wasp-waisted summer.

III

Hatch

dragonfly nymphs crouched on six spindly legs
    small tannish tanks deployed single file on our anchor line
        a transit for these crawling creatures up from the shallows

while we swam then sunned like dazed and blinking lizards
    enchanted, hands quiet on kneecaps
        our naturalist eyes trained on them

those nymphs, Escher-like, in ascending
    order of metamorphosis, drying hard, extravagant
        their final molt, lake bottom scurry and jet finished

Later days of sitting with you, your breathing so like labor
    my clasp tightening on your loosening, and late one night
        I tried to remember those few hours of effort

to birth themselves (to some greater glory?)
    in that sun-muddled limbo between water and sky
        when I wanted to say, *dear ones, you hatch like spirits*

dear ones, a miracle–even then we understood it wasn't
    nor was *hatch* the right term, but I needed solace
        some earthly allegory of multi-folded nature–

those few lines of electric blue shock—slow motion vaulting
    through shoulder blades of old skin—clinging a moment
        to their own emptied selves while their huge prismatic eyes

focus on mosaics of flickering motion, their ancient engines fire
    wings dry and throb into position, and they rise—
        each an exclamation point stunned blue.

Flame

When a flame appearing to float outside above a fence
is actually the reflection of my sister's candle,

burning in her memory on the kitchen counter.
When it's doubling through the double-pane window,

floating in the center of the willow bush.
We left you with a close family friend saying the rosary.

I couldn't stay. When the flame is the most real aspect
of this late September landscape.

Gentle yellow flame. Now like two small arms waving.
When I move to the left, it is framed

by a canopy of late white clematis.
When this is all I can do.

Waking to Grief

Barely audible
creeping from the corner

slight as accretion
in a crystal of salt

dead weight of wrapped linens
on limbs

prickling of salt
on the skin

and palest light accruing
between the shade

and dust
on the sill

East Woods

As sleet sifts like sugar through these woods
where we liked to run, I think I see you
through the waking trees,

hear you sigh in the understory
like small exhaling twigs
but how could I know for certain.

Are you hidden in a lichen robe?
Could those hands be yours, signaling
in frozen patterns on this rocky ledge?

No. Not like you, never a Klimt figure lost
in the background of a complicated couch,
busily sitting, lost in pattern, a vapid stare.

Oh, but now I glimpse your running figure
like stuttering film through sprockets of trees,
black and white, grainy and granular.

Yes! Much better! Running through
glazed and snapping witch hazel, flavor
on your tongue, licking your fingers, laughing.

Looking up from bleak headlines at these friable trees

and earth parched beneath an overburdened sky
sky like a mother with five children
and no money coming in

All day I've been building a chassis for thought
but the innards are at the shop for repair
touch the keys and there's no give, no give–

(*chassé chassé* so bleak the day) no give
with this word-salad mind, its slivers
of dreams and bad news

its hunger and heady belief
that sky is its hand mirror
handmaiden, mother

And when sky pulls close her stony coat
fragments spill from holes in her pockets
raining down on me like meteors

April Accounting

Good Friday and Passover fall together this year
        so business is dead. I observe neither,

descendant of pragmatic people, of Lithuanian dance bands
        and practiced meagerness, down in this lakeside warehouse

having time to unpack and take inventory of the spring arrival,
        pulling sheets of glass from fork-lifted, straw-filled crates,

listening to music, to a raccoon in the rafters, rain on the tin roof,
        while back home sweatshirts and jeans piled on the floor

turn feral. Useless ruminations that stumble like beasts of burden,
        with their downcast mouths and alert eyes, step aside–

worries of building codes, gentrification, rising costs give way
        to dreams of green sunsets, fresh laundry, hedged bets,

cleaning and recording sheets of seedy amber, gold-pink,
        midnight blue, watery teal. It's not so bad to be bathed

in color when dark is falling. Glass reflecting, crates emptying,
        neat columns of numbers lengthening

while run-off pours down streets from the pretty hill town above,
        and trucks wash clean through this rainy street.

You Will Feel a Pinch

Then a burn.
Fires blacken
southern California.
The polar vortex paws
its white way down
from the melting north,
freezing the Midwest.

Sometimes averages
are useless.
This is not the place
to conflate personal frostbite
with the fate of the earth,
even if a friend's bipolar swing
seems to call for it.
Here frigid. There burn.

But this announced plunge and pitch
with its false sense of stability
doesn't convince me. And you?
We are black and blue from it.

Prayer

Not a nightjar but a common jay
flits and screeches through the shallow night.
Not a savior but a charlatan
places his hands on the heads of the people.

Let magic return this paltry night.
Let it jar us out of our paralysis,
we who want and wait,
we who grieve and regret.

Let regrets become egrets
that brood in the marsh
and overwashed grief wear itself out.
Let morning arrive with fresh pollen.

What the Rock Said

Weight is challenging, I admit,
but nothing compared to my
penchant for change.

Just as you have a firm grip,
it's then I become petulant
or cruel as a kitchen knife

or slick and sweaty,
your face against mine,
or abrupt as an avalanche.

Yes, it's true I preserve
these nightmares in heaviness,
rolling back at you always.

We both know
you are all push
and I letting go.

Now, though, I feel
your hands slip,
your feet give way,
and I am afraid for you.

While you were sleeping

all the old meanings swept
from their moorings, the meanness,
all the weapons, buffoonery,
your wounded heart.

Worry warrior, wake up and drift with me
in soft and softer shades of news.
See, we're okay—it's only that this boat,
roused by some bellwether,
is sliding out into vast day.

Remember the baby's excited gibberish,
pointing at each picture-book page
then smiling—the way I do
at any happy, hopeful ending?

Because all that hard-luck green,
the palpitations,
all the tense smiles, the wet palms—
we've left them on the dock
with our shoes.

Whitecaps like white curtains
whisper secrets of the wind
come to cool, not to chill,
oh, breath of some large creature
who loves us.

Questions While Deep-Cleaning the Desk

1

Early morning when
I walk into a room of
deflating Mylar butterflies
now sunken to waist high–
What were we celebrating?
And what significance?
Do all great events deflate?
Say events pass, they pass
and are replaced
by other events.
Right now I'm a giant
among makeshift clouds.

2

I thought I was your queen and you my faithful subjects.
My own biome.
But who's making that ruckus behind my heart?
Uprising in the lower lobe of the left lung.
Coughing doesn't help, is just a symptom.

We're made of many millions of cells and good bacteria–
how many millions did he say, Sam Harris?
How much do bacteria make our choices?

What about the renegades beating their drums?
Do they realize they may destroy
the whole world of self? Do they care?

    3

I knew it would take something
like this to clean the desk:
impending death. Little time left
to pay attention to my *self*
as in author of a life,
with a narrator flawed but unintentional,
as I note the bills waiting to be paid,
the piano to be dusted and played.

    4

Soon you'll be able to clone
your husband with a hair
from the one suit coat
you haven't yet given away
at the back of the closet.

And the clone....How fast
does he grow up?
What if he doesn't fall in love
with you this time around?
Or you with him?
What do you do with him then?

More Gray

No more clear lines delineating
this from that, please.
More gray, please.

Black in its smug certainty
blocks out all that is becoming,
hesitant, wavering.

White, glib tundra of *shhh*,
exhorts complete
and final silence.
More gray, please.

That incessant lake gray.
The gray of distant rain shafts.
A blending of all and nothing
is not a cancellation.

A hue shimmering at the horizon?
Perhaps some shade of primal rust to start.
This time more slowly, please.

Hammocked and Unstrung

Here I lie at time's keen edge
somewhere between lithe
and spry, but neither violin
nor nervous wreck.

Long after a flock of white ducks
with Crayola yellow legs
dipped for weeds,
I float above the surface of the past.

Recently released from mirrored spaces,
from turtle depths of night, from
days of hurried reflection,

days of *now, what now,*
days of unvaried syntax,
as if in airports and endless travel.

Days of travail and sickness,
heart-stopping news close and afar,
adrenaline pumping faster,
illusory decisions I thought best.

Then time moved on
to benevolent luck,
gathered its dice
and threw two sixes.

Now a white whippet in a red coat
has just licked clean
a plate of golden crumbs
and stretches next to me
in this bright green hammock.

Story

A summer night with no need for particulars, but for the bare limbed
      sway of things. Dishes clattering in sinks, a radio being tuned.

A neighborhood of modest streets and bungalows. Paper lanterns
      strung through apple trees. Filtered candlelight

around a garden table in a deep back yard. Remnants of a summer banquet.
      Lightly clad figures lean in to hear a story rise to its conclusion.

A crescendo of laughter, a cacophonous bouquet
      of tone and register, spills through the neighborhood

where a passing walker with her dog catches that essential pleasure,
      a story in its setting, its rise and fall, feels its thrill, even without the words.

Windblown Sonnet for Brass

Sky ajar with off-key riffs of Canada geese,
       their formations blown awry by heavy winds

as they shoulder their way less south than east,
         honking homeward-bound, those drunk musicians.

Below, finished tomato vines staked with white rags on poles
        resemble wounded soldiers staggering home from the Civil War.

Nearby among the churn of faded leaves, autumn mums, the yellow of yolks,
       jolt like cheerful nurses at a deathbed beneath the flying squawk.

Today we plant yet more spring bulbs, and more,
       early-blooming tulips, parrot-orange, ruffled red;

We shout through cupped hands beneath the branches' roar,
         and turn to catch each other's wind-strewn words.

Everywhere, this lurch and flash. Each time we jab four holes each section,
       a shock of phosphorescent roots thrusts in every possible direction.

Free Will with Small Yellow Truck

For half an hour I've been speaking in the voice of a small yellow truck, whose wheels move across the coffee table at my will, just as my will moves at the whim of this two-year-old prime mover, who, I've just read yesterday, is scripted by the laws of physics, as he learns these laws through his moving vehicle, a red bulldozer with large black treads rolling next to and sometimes over my small yellow truck. I've been speaking as a truck for so long, my appearance has transformed. I back up and turn. Neuroscientists say *no* to free will. Shakespeare says we're merely players, his many sad twists of fate, coincidences, happy and tragic. Will I ever write again? It won't be my fault if I don't. I'm busy following the bulldozer who's driving slowly across the coffee table into a cardboard garage. I park next to him. But not for long. Because motion is endlessly fascinating. I've just forgotten why. I want to glance at his intense little face, but if I lose my place, will I stall? I follow him to the other end of the coffee table, where a blue box with a tasseled lid reigns. He will park there and want to open it.

Acknowledgments

Grateful acknowledgment is made to the editors of the following journals and websites where these poems first appeared:

Alaska Quarterly Review: "Free Will with Small Yellow Truck"

Bellevue Literary Journal: "You Will Feel a Pinch"

Broad Street: "Home Security," "Package," "While you were sleeping," "Night Mending," "A Hypochondriac's Guide to the Body," "Notes from a Capricious Correspondent"

Iodine Poetry: "Prayer"

Midwest Quarterly Review: "Hatch"

New England Association of Teachers of English: Earlier version of "Ockham, Excommunicate"

The New Yorker: "About Muscle"

Nimrod International Journal: "Looking up from bleak headlines at these friable trees," "The Sum of Its Parts"

The Pedestal Magazine: "Foreign Cities"

Poetry East: "New England Summer"

Spillway: "Shift"

Page-turner: *This Year in Poetry: Highlights of 2014 (newyorker.com)*: "About Muscle"

Círculo de Poesía: reprint and translation into Spanish of "About Muscle" and "Foreign Cities"

Thanks to Francisco Larios for his fine translations for *Círculo de Poesía*.

Deep gratitude to the talented poets with whom I have worked over the years: Anna Blackmer, Alison Moncrief Bromage, Sue D. Burton, Judith Chalmer, Anne Damrosch, Nora Mitchell, Florence McCloud, Angela Patten, Alison Prine, Bonnie Shand, Emily Skoler and Joan White.

Thanks to David Huddle and Stephen Cramer for reading my manuscript and offering suggestions.

To Louise Stoll, much gratitude for her support of this project.

To Mark Pendergrast for his editing skills and care in fine-tuning this collection, and to Lin Stone of Wind Ridge Books, for her kindness and skill in making this book a reality.

Thanks to Kimberly Boyce, Toronto singer-songwriter, (Kimberlyboyce.com), for her soulful arrangement of "About Muscle."

Special thanks to my son, Jeremy Fortin, for his cover art and author photo.

Thanks to my niece, Riley McAlpine Barthold, for her support and care.

And to my husband, Larry Ribbecke, deep gratitude for all his love and support.

www.ingramcontent.com/pod-product-compliance
Lightning Source LLC
Chambersburg PA
CBHW050455110426
42743CB00017B/3373